CONQUER YOUR EMOTIONS

Tested And Trusted Practical Guide to Conquer
Negativity and Manage your Emotions

PETER EIKHUEMELP

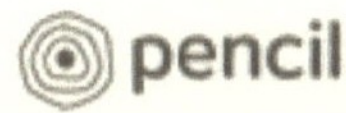

ISBN 978-93-5883-109-2
© PETER EIKHUEMELP 2023

Published in India 2023 by Pencil

A brand of
One Point Six Technologies Pvt. Ltd.
Unit no. 26, Ground Floor, Building A1,
Wadala Truck Terminal Road,
Near Post Office, Antop Hill, Mumbai - 400037
E connect@thepencilapp.com
W www.thepencilapp.com

DISCLAIMER: *The opinions expressed in this book are those of the authors and do not purport to reflect the views of the Publisher.*

Author biography

Peter Eikhuemelo is an accomplished writer known for their captivating storytelling and thought-provoking narratives. With a passion for exploring the complexities of human relationships and societal dynamics, he has crafted a diverse body of work that encompasses various genres, including fiction, romance, and contemporary literature. Their ability to create compelling characters and delve into the depths of human emotions has garnered critical acclaim and a loyal readership. Drawing inspiration from personal experiences, cultural observations, and a keen understanding of human nature, [Author's Name] weaves intricate tales that resonate with readers worldwide. Their works offer profound insights, challenging readers to question societal norms, explore the intricacies of love and identity, and contemplate the human condition. Through their evocative prose and ability to capture the essence of the human experience, he continues to leave a lasting impact on the literary world.

CONTENTS

Preface

READING THIS BOOK

Reading "How to Conquer Your Emotions" is an immersive and transformative experience that offers a comprehensive roadmap to mastering your emotional landscape. This concise yet impactful guide is designed to empower readers with practical tools and insights, providing them with the necessary skills to navigate life's emotional challenges with grace and self-awareness.

Self-Discovery: It will encourage readers to embark on a journey of self-discovery, gaining a deeper understanding of their emotions, triggers, and behavioral patterns. Through introspective exercises, readers can uncover the roots of their emotional responses and identify areas for personal growth.

Emotional Intelligence: "How to Conquer Your Emotions" delves into the concept of emotional intelligence, emphasizing its importance in daily life. Readers learn how to cultivate emotional intelligence, enabling them to navigate relationships, make better decisions, and effectively communicate their feelings.

Mindfulness Practices: This literature introduces readers to mindfulness techniques that aid in recognizing and embracing emotions without judgment. By practicing mindfulness, readers can develop a heightened sense of emotional awareness and respond to situations in a more balanced and composed manner.

Regulation and Coping Strategies: With a focus on practicality, the book equips readers with various strategies for regulating emotions and coping with stress, anxiety, and overwhelming feelings. These tools empower readers to foster emotional resilience and maintain equilibrium during challenging circumstances.

Personal Growth: It inspires readers to view emotions as allies in personal growth rather than obstacles. By harnessing the power of their emotional experiences, readers can tap into their full potential and lead more meaningful, authentic lives.

Empathy and Compassion: The book emphasizes the importance of empathy and compassion in fostering healthier relationships. Readers learn how to understand and validate others' emotions, leading to deeper connections and improved communication.

Sustainable Change: By providing practical advice and evidence-based insights, the book ensures that the transformational effects are long-lasting. Readers are encouraged to integrate the lessons into their daily lives, ensuring a sustainable positive change in their emotional well-being.

Reading "How to Conquer Your Emotions" is an invitation to take charge of your emotional journey, enabling you to embrace emotions as a powerful force for personal growth and empowerment. Whether you're seeking to improve relationships, manage stress, or simply lead a more balanced life, it equips you with the necessary tools to navigate emotions with resilience, mindfulness, and authenticity. It is a call to action to embark on a life-changing quest towards emotional mastery and a brighter, more fulfilling future.

Introduction

Welcome to "Conquer Your Emotions," a transformative guide designed to empower you to take control of your emotional well-being and find inner harmony. In today's fast-paced and challenging world, emotions can often feel overwhelming, leading to stress, anxiety, and hindered personal growth. This book is your key to understanding and discipline your emotions, allowing you to navigate life's ups and downs with resilience and clarity.

Through a blend of cutting-edge psychological research, practical techniques, and relatable anecdotes, "Conquer Your Emotions" offers a comprehensive roadmap for emotional self-awareness and regulation. Whether it's managing anger, coping with fear, or fostering positive emotions, this book provides you with the tools and strategies to embrace emotional intelligence and lead a more fulfilling life.

By delving into the core principles of emotional intelligence and exploring various mindfulness practices, you'll learn how to identify triggers, respond mindfully, and develop healthier coping mechanisms. Throughout this journey, you'll discover that emotions are not obstacles or hinderances to overcome but powerful allies that can guide you towards personal growth and deeper connections with others.

Join us as we embark on this empowering exploration of emotions, empowering you to become the master of your emotional landscape. Are you ready to embark on a path of self-discovery and emotional empowerment? Let "Conquer Your Emotions" be your trusted companion as we navigate the fascinating terrain of human emotions together. Let's begin the journey to unlock the true potential that lies within you!

i

REASON FOR THE BOOK

In contemporary fast-paced and demanding world, emotional turbulence is an all-too-common challenge that many individuals confront. Why this book "Conquer Your Emotions" stems from the pressing need to provide a practical and empowering guide for readers to navigate their emotional landscapes with confidence and self-awareness. The objective of this book is to address the crucial importance of emotional intelligence and its impact on personal well-being, relationships, and overall success in life. By delving into the science behind emotions and offering actionable strategies, "Conquer Your Emotions" seeks to equip readers with the tools they need to understand, manage, and leverage their emotions effectively.

With a focus on mindfulness practices, psychological insights, and real-life examples, the book empowers readers to:

Know and Understand Emotions: The book helps readers recognize various emotions and the underlying causes behind them, fostering a deeper sense of self-awareness.

Regulate Emotional Responses: By exploring practical techniques, readers can develop healthier ways of responding to emotional triggers, avoiding impulsive reactions.

Cultivate Emotional Intelligence:"Conquer Your Emotions" guides readers in developing emotional intelligence, leading to improved decision-making, communication, and empathy.

Promote Mental Resilience: Through empowering exercises, the book aids readers in building resilience, enabling them to bounce back from challenges and setbacks.

Develop Relationships: By understanding their emotions and those of others, readers can establish more meaningful and harmonious connections in their personal and professional lives.

Achieve Personal Growth: By mastering their emotional landscape, readers can unlock their true potential and embark on a journey of self-discovery and growth.

Overall, "Conquer Your Emotions" serves as a valuable resource for individuals seeking to harness the power of emotional intelligence, leading to a more fulfilling and balanced life. It is a call to action for readers to take charge of their emotional well-being and embrace emotions as a catalyst for personal growth and empowerment.

PART 1 WHOLE OF EMOTIONS

WHOLE OF EMOTIONS

In the symphony of the soul, emotions dance like ethereal notes, weaving a tapestry of experiences that shape the very essence of humanity. This classical detail delves into the captivating interplay of the whole of emotions, illuminating the intricacies of joy, sorrow, love, anger, and everything in between those colors the canvas of human existence.

I. **The Melody of Joy**

Joy, like a brilliant sunrise, awakens the heart to the beauty of life. It dances in the laughter of children, the warmth of reunions, and the triumph of accomplishments. The melody of joy lifts the spirit, infusing days with a sense of lightness, and reminding us that life's true treasures reside in the simple moments of happiness.

II. **The Aria of Sorrow**

Sorrow, a mournful aria that echoes in the chambers of the heart, unveils the depth of our capacity to feel. It flows with tears of loss, the ache of parting, and the weight of life's inevitable farewells. The aria of sorrow invites us to embrace vulnerability, acknowledging that our tears water the seeds of compassion and empathy.

III. **The Harmonies of Love**

Love, with its multifaceted harmonies, binds souls together and nourishes the human spirit. It sings in the tender moments shared between loved ones, in the sacrifices made for others' happiness, and in the profound connections that transcend time and distance. The harmonies of love resonate within us, reminding us of our capacity to give and receive the purest form of affection.

IV. **The Crescendo of Anger**

Anger, like a powerful crescendo, surges forth, demanding to be heard and acknowledged. It can spark change, defend boundaries, and propel us to confront injustice. But like the tempestuous sea, anger must be harnessed with wisdom, for its force can be destructive if not tempered by understanding and compassion.

V. **The Symphony of Compassion**

Compassion, a symphony of empathy and understanding, resonates in the human heart. It prompts us to extend a helping hand to those in need, to alleviate suffering, and to walk in another's shoes. The symphony of compassion unites us in our shared humanity, reminding us that we are not alone in our struggles and triumphs.

VI. **The Overture of Courage**

Courage, an inspiring overture that emboldens the spirit, accompanies us through life's trials and tribulations. It is the catalyst for change, the force that propels us forward despite fear and uncertainty. The overture of courage teaches us that growth and transformation often emerge from the very challenges we face.

VII. **The Cadence of Gratitude**

Gratitude, a soothing cadence that calms the soul, reminds us of life's abundant blessings. It resounds in the little things we often take for granted - a warm embrace, a shared meal, or a sunlit morning. The cadence of gratitude encourages us to savor life's moments, acknowledging the preciousness of each breath.

In the symphony of life, the whole of emotions orchestrate a grand opus, reflecting the myriad facets of the human experience. Each emotion plays its unique role, adding depth and richness to our journey. From the highest crescendos of joy to the soft cadences of gratitude, and everything in between, this symphony of emotions weaves the tapestry of our lives, reminding us of the beauty and complexity of being human. By embracing the whole of emotions with grace and introspection, we learn to harmonize the symphony of the soul, creating a melodic masterpiece that resonates throughout eternity.

WAYS YOUR EMOTIONS ARE CONTROLLED BY YOUR SURVIVAL MECHANISM

Comprehending the intricate relationship between emotions and survival mechanisms is a fundamental aspect of human psychology. This comprehensive exploration delves into the various ways in which our emotions are intricately linked to our ancient survival instincts, shaping our behaviors and responses to the world around us.

The Evolutionary Roots of Emotions: Exploring deep into our evolutionary history, this study reveals how emotions emerged as crucial survival tools to help our ancestors navigate a hazardous environment. By examining the roles of fear, anger, joy, and sadness, we uncover how these emotions evolved to protect and aid our species.

Fight or Flight Response: One of the most crucial survival mechanisms, the fight or flight response, triggers a surge of adrenaline and cortisol in the face of perceived threats. This investigations highlights how our emotions activate this response, preparing us to confront or flee from danger in the most efficient way possible.

Emotional Memory and Learning: Our emotions play a pivotal role in forming and reinforcing memories, especially those associated with survival experiences. By understanding how emotions influence memory and learning processes, we gain insight into how our past experiences shape our emotional responses in the present.

Control of Stress: The survival mechanism deeply impacts how we regulate stress. This investigation explores the complex interplay between emotions and stress hormones, shedding light on how our emotional states influence our ability to cope with challenging situations.

Emotional Contagion and Social Bonding: Experiencing emotions is not limited to individuals; it extends to our social connections as well. This research explores emotional contagion and the mechanisms by which we synchronize emotions with others, fostering social bonding and cooperation—an essential aspect of human survival.

Decision-Making and Risk Assessment: Emotions significantly influence our decision-making processes, as they help us assess risks and rewards. This exploration uncovers how emotions guide our choices, ensuring we make decisions that increase our chances of survival and well-being.

Emotional Regulation and Resilience: Understanding the interplay between emotions and survival mechanisms provides insights into emotional regulation and resilience. We examine how developing emotional intelligence empowers individuals to navigate adversity and build greater psychological strength.

The Role of Contemporary Society: While our survival mechanisms served us well in ancient times, modern society poses unique challenges. We discuss how the same survival mechanisms can sometimes lead to maladaptive responses in today's world and explore strategies to adapt positively to a rapidly changing environment.

By shedding light on the ways our emotions are intricately controlled by our survival mechanism, this study offers valuable insights into human behavior, decision-making, and interpersonal dynamics. It is an invitation to explore the deep-seated connection between our evolutionary past and present emotional experiences, inspiring a more profound understanding of ourselves and the world we inhabit. Moreover, armed with this knowledge, readers can harness their emotional responses effectively, fostering personal growth, and thriving in an increasingly complex and dynamic world.

WHO IS THE EGO?

In the realm of psychology, the term "ego" refers to a crucial aspect of the human psyche and identity. Coined by Sigmund Freud, the renowned Austrian psychoanalyst, the concept of the ego is a fundamental element of psychoanalytic theory. It plays a central role in shaping an individual's thoughts, behaviors, and interactions with the world.

The ego is one of the three components of the psychic apparatus proposed by Freud, alongside the id and the superego. Each of these components represents different aspects of the mind and operates with distinct motivations.

The Ego's Function and Characteristics:

The ego is the executive part of the psyche, responsible for mediating between the instinctual, impulsive desires of the id and the moral and societal constraints imposed by the superego. It acts as a decision-maker, aiming to find a balance between the conflicting demands of these two opposing forces.

Characterized by rationality, logical thinking, and reality-testing, the ego enables individuals to navigate the complexities of the external world effectively. It helps in making choices that consider both immediate gratification (from the id) and the long-term consequences and social norms (from the superego).

Ego Defense Mechanisms:

One of the significant functions of the ego is to protect the individual from anxiety and distress caused by conflicting desires or threatening thoughts. To cope with internal conflicts, the ego employs defense mechanisms—psychological strategies that unconsciously distort reality. These mechanisms help alleviate emotional discomfort and maintain psychological equilibrium.

Common ego defense mechanisms include denial (refusing to accept unpleasant truths), repression (pushing distressing memories into the unconscious), and projection (attributing one's undesirable feelings onto others). While these mechanisms serve to protect the individual in the short term, they can also hinder personal growth and self-awareness if overused.

Ego Development and Childhood:

According to Freud, the formation of the ego begins in early childhood. Initially, an infant's mind is primarily driven by the id's instinctual desires. As the child interacts with caregivers and the environment, they gradually learn to navigate the external world and adapt to societal expectations. This process helps shape the ego and establish a sense of self.

Early childhood experiences, especially the quality of parental care and the nature of early relationships, can significantly influence ego development. Positive, nurturing experiences contribute to the emergence of a well-functioning ego, while neglect or trauma may lead to ego vulnerabilities or maladaptive patterns of behavior.

Ego in Contemporary Psychology:

While Freud's psychoanalytic theory laid the foundation for understanding the ego, contemporary psychology has expanded and refined these concepts. The study of ego psychology and other psychodynamic theories continues to be relevant in understanding human behavior and mental processes.

In addition to psychoanalysis, the term "ego" is also commonly used in everyday language to describe an individual's self-image, self-esteem, or sense of self-importance. In this sense, the ego refers to a person's perception of themselves and their place in the world.

In conclusion, the ego is a crucial element of the human psyche, serving as the mediator between instinctual desires and societal norms. It allows individuals to navigate the complexities of life, develop a sense of self, and cope with internal conflicts. Understanding the ego's role and its development provides valuable insights into human behavior, relationships, and personal growth.

THE FABRIC OF EMOTIONS

In the symphony of human experience, emotions are the intricate melodies that resonate deep within our souls. This classical exploration delves into the fabric of emotions, unveiling the essence of these profound inner experiences that shape our perceptions, actions, and connections with the world.

The Essence of Emotions:

"The Fabric of Emotions" seeks to unravel the essence of these intangible phenomena that color the human experience. It explores into the question of what emotions truly are—raw, primal responses or complex cognitive processes—and reflects on their role in our daily lives.

The Psychological and Physiological Dimensions:

This exploration navigates the duality of emotions by examining both their psychological and physiological dimensions. It delves into the intricate interplay between the mind and the body, exploring how emotions arise from a combination of neural activity, hormones, and cognitive processes.

Universality and Cultural Variability:

Emotions are a universal aspect of the human experience, yet they also bear the stamp of cultural influences. This exploration celebrates the common emotional threads that bind humanity together while acknowledging the cultural nuances that give rise to diverse emotional expressions across societies.

The Evolutionary Tapestry:

Unraveling the nature of emotions entails exploring their evolutionary origins. By examining the adaptive functions of emotions in our ancestors' survival and social bonding, we gain insights into how these emotional threads have been woven into the fabric of human evolution.

The Language of Emotions:

"The Fabric of Emotions" investigates the language of emotions—the ways in which we express and communicate our inner feelings. Whether through facial expressions, body language, or verbal cues, emotions form a universal language that enables us to connect with others on a profound, emotional level.

The Complex Interplay:

Emotions seldom exist in isolation; they intertwine and influence each other, creating a complex symphony of feelings within us. This exploration dissects the intricate interplay between emotions, shedding light on how one emotional experience can trigger cascading responses.

Emotions and Decision-Making:

Understanding the nature of emotions involves examining their impact on decision-making processes. This exploration reflects on how emotions can influence our choices, guiding us towards actions or hindering rational decision-making when emotions override logic.

Emotional Intelligence and Regulation:

The fabric of emotions extends to our capacity for emotional intelligence and regulation. By delving into the art of understanding and managing our emotions, we uncover strategies for enhancing self-awareness, empathy, and emotional well-being.

It is an invitation to embark on a journey of self-discovery and exploration, fostering a deeper understanding of these enigmatic aspects of our human essence. It celebrates the beauty and complexity of emotions, inviting us to embrace their transformative power and guiding us to find harmony within ourselves and with others. As we unravel the symphony of emotions within us, we gain a profound appreciation for the intricate tapestry of human existence and the universal language that connects us all.

PART II WHAT EMOTIONS ARE

Emotions are intricate psychological and physical experiences that are essential to the human experience. They play a major role in how we see, understand, and react to the environment around us every day. Emotions are multidimensional experiences that affect our thoughts, activities, and general well-being; they are not just ephemeral feelings. Navigating the complexities of human nature and promoting stronger emotional intelligence require a solid understanding of what emotions are and how they work.

Emotions can be characterized as a collection of interrelated psychological and physiological reactions to both internal and external events. They result from a person's subjective assessment and interpretation of facts, circumstances, and ideas. Emotions are not just one type of experience; they also include a wide range of body reactions, thoughts, and sensations that are frequently connected and dependent on one another.

Emotional components:

The following elements of emotions all add to their complexity:

The first is the cognitive component, which includes the mental operations linked to emotions like perception, focus, and appraisal. It encompasses the way people understand and provide meaning to experiences or events, which causes emotional reactions.

b. **Physiological Aspect**: Different physiological reactions occur in the body as a result of emotions. Changes in heart rate, breathing rate, hormone release, and muscle tension are a few examples. The "fight or flight" reaction, created to get the body ready to react to perceived dangers, includes several physical changes.

c. **Expressive Component:**Facial expressions, body language, and vocal intonation are frequently used to convey emotions. Others can learn about a person's emotional condition through these nonverbal indicators.

d. **Subjective Feelings:**The actual feelings, such as joy, rage, fear, sadness, and more, are included in the subjective experience of emotions. Depending on the circumstance and personal preferences, these emotions might range in intensity and length.

The Commonality of Emotions

The idea that emotions are universal across cultures leads to the conclusion that certain emotional manifestations and experiences are possessed by all people. For instance, people from many cultural backgrounds can recognize and comprehend the basic facial expressions of emotions including happiness, sadness, anger, fear, surprise, and disgust.

Emotional Function:

Multiple essential roles that emotions play in ensuring human existence and wellbeing include:

a. **Adaptation:**By dictating actions and reactions, emotions assist people in adapting to their surroundings. For instance, while joy can reinforce pleasant experiences and promote repetition, fear can cause people to avoid potentially dangerous circumstances.

b. **Nonverbal communication:**Emotions are a type of nonverbal communication that let others know about a person's feelings and intentions. Cooperation and social bonding are aided by this.

c. **Decision-Making**: Emotions affect decision-making by offering a useful assessment of circumstances based on prior experiences and

d. **Memory Formation:**Strong emotional content in events or experiences might help memory consolidation, making them more remembered.

In the end, emotions are complex and important aspects of human life that include a variety of expressive, physiological, and psychological elements. They have a significant impact on how we see and move through the world, influencing our thoughts, behaviors, and interpersonal interactions. For preserving mental health, promoting empathy, and creating deep connections with people, it is crucial to understand emotions and to build emotional intelligence. Emotions are an essential component of human nature that enrich our lives and add to the complex tapestry of human experience.

HOW SLEEP AFFECTS YOUR MOOD

Sleep is a fundamental aspect of human physiology, and its impact on our mood and emotional well-being is profound. This comprehensive exploration delves into the intricate relationship between sleep and mood, shedding light on how the quality and quantity of our sleep directly influence our emotional state.

Sleep and Emotional Control:
Adequate sleep plays a crucial role in emotional regulation, helping us maintain stable and balanced moods. When we

sleep, the brain processes and consolidates emotional experiences, allowing us to better cope with stress and challenges the following day. Insufficient sleep, on the other hand, can lead to heightened emotional reactivity and decreased resilience in the face of emotional stimuli.

Impact on Mood Disorders:

Sleep disturbances can exacerbate preexisting mood disorders, such as depression and anxiety. Research shows that individuals with insomnia or disrupted sleep patterns are more susceptible to experiencing symptoms of these mood disorders. Addressing sleep problems can be an essential component of managing and treating such conditions.

Sleep Deprivation and Irritability:

A lack of sleep can lead to irritability and a short temper. When we are sleep-deprived, our ability to regulate emotions diminishes, and we may find ourselves more easily agitated or frustrated. Additionally, sleep-deprived individuals are more likely to experience heightened emotional reactions to otherwise minor stressors.

Relationship Between Sleep and Positive Emotions:

Quality sleep not only regulates negative emotions but also enhances positive emotions. Studies have shown that individuals who get sufficient sleep tend to experience more joy, contentment, and optimism, while sleep deprivation can lead to a decrease in positive emotions and an overall lower mood.

The Role of REM Sleep:

Rapid Eye Movement (REM) sleep, a stage of deep sleep associated with dreaming, plays a critical role in emotional processing. During REM sleep, the brain processes emotional memories and experiences, facilitating emotional integration and understanding. Disruptions in REM sleep can lead to emotional dysregulation and increased vulnerability to mood disturbances.

Sleep and Emotional Memory:

Sleep is essential for memory consolidation, including emotional memories. During sleep, the brain processes and stores emotional information, allowing us to remember and learn from emotionally charged experiences. Insufficient or disrupted sleep can impair this process, potentially leading to difficulties in processing emotions and emotional memories.

The Bidirectional Relationship:

The relationship between sleep and mood is bidirectional, meaning that not only does sleep affect our mood, but our mood can also impact our sleep. Negative emotions, stress, and anxiety can disrupt sleep patterns, creating a cycle where poor sleep leads to worsened mood, and vice versa.

Finally, the connection between sleep and mood is intricate and multi-faceted. Adequate, restorative sleep is crucial for emotional regulation, positive mood, and overall mental well-being. Conversely, sleep disturbances can lead to heightened emotional reactivity, worsened mood disorders, and impaired emotional processing. Understanding the significant impact of sleep on our emotional health empowers us to prioritize healthy sleep habits and embrace the transformative power of a good night's rest.

CONTROLLING YOUR EMOTIONS USING YOUR BODY

The affinity between the body and emotions is a powerful and intricate one. This comprehensive exploration delves into the fascinating ways in which our physical actions and body language can be harnessed to influence, regulate, and even transform our emotional states.

The Mind-Body Connection:

The mind-body connection reveals that our emotions and bodily responses are intimately linked. When we experience different emotions, our bodies respond with specific physiological changes. Conversely, deliberately manipulating our bodies can influence the emotions we feel. Understanding this connection allows us to explore the potential of using our body to control and shape our emotional experiences.

The Power of Body Language:

Body language plays a central role in emotional communication. Subtle movements, gestures, and postures can convey emotions to others and even impact our internal emotional states. Adopting open and expansive body language can promote feelings of confidence and positivity, while closed and constricted postures may amplify feelings of fear or sadness.

The Role of Facial Expressions:

Facial expressions are a primary means of emotional expression. Smiling, for instance, can trigger the release of feel-good neurotransmitters like endorphins and serotonin, leading to an improvement in mood. Conversely, frowning or tensing facial muscles can intensify feelings of anger or stress. By consciously controlling our facial expressions, we can influence our emotional experiences.

Breathing Techniques and Emotional Regulation:

Breathing exercises are powerful tools for emotional regulation. Deep, slow breaths activate the body's parasympathetic nervous system, promoting relaxation and reducing stress. Shallow or rapid breathing, on the other hand, can increase feelings of anxiety and tension. Employing intentional breathing techniques allows us to modulate our emotional responses and find inner calm.

Body-Mind Feedback Loop:

A fascinating aspect of controlling emotions through the body is the body-mind feedback loop. Emotions can trigger physical responses, but changing our physical state can also influence our emotions. For example, engaging in physical activities or exercise can elevate mood through the release of endorphins, dopamine, and other "feel-good" chemicals.

Posture and Confidence:

Adopting a confident posture, such as standing tall with shoulders back, not only communicates confidence to others but also fosters feelings of empowerment within ourselves. This phenomenon, known as "power posing," can positively impact self-esteem and self-assurance.

Using Movement to Shift Emotions:

Physical movement can serve as a conduit for emotional expression and release. Engaging in activities like dancing, yoga, or even simply going for a walk can channel and transform emotions, offering a healthy outlet for processing and managing emotional experiences.

In the end, the connection between the body and emotions is a powerful tool for emotional regulation and transformation. By becoming aware of how our physical actions and body language influence our emotions, we can harness this relationship to navigate our emotional landscape with intention and resilience. Empowering ourselves to control or influence our emotions using our body allows us to cultivate emotional well-being, enhance our relationships, and embrace the transformative potential of body-mind integration.

CONTROLLING YOUR EMOTIONS USING YOUR THOUGHTS

The process of controlling or influencing One's thought is termed emotional regulation It involves the conscious effort to manage emotions and responses to various situations effectively. While emotions are a natural and essential aspect of being human, they can sometimes become overwhelming or hinder our ability to make rational decisions. By understanding and harnessing the power of our thoughts, individuals can gain greater control over their emotions, leading to improved mental well-being and healthier relationships.

Recognizing Emotions: Emotions are complex and diverse, ranging from joy and happiness to fear, anger, and sadness. They are the product of a combination of biological, psychological, and environmental factors. These emotions can be triggered by external events or internal thoughts and beliefs. Acknowledging that emotions are natural responses to stimuli is the first step towards emotional regulation. Cognitive Appraisal: One of the fundamental ways thoughts influence emotions is through cognitive appraisal. Cognitive appraisal refers to the process of interpreting and evaluating a situation, which subsequently influences how an individual feels about it. For instance, if someone interprets a challenging situation as a threat, they may experience fear or anxiety. However, viewing the same situation as an opportunity for growth may generate feelings of excitement or determination.

Cognitive Restructuring: Cognitive restructuring is a technique used to challenge and modify negative thought patterns or cognitive distortions. These distortions can lead to exaggerated emotional responses. By actively identifying and reframing negative thoughts, individuals can shift their emotions towards a more positive and balanced state. For example, instead of catastrophizing an upcoming event, such as a job interview, cognitive restructuring encourages focusing on the potential positive outcomes.

Awareness and Meditation: Practicing mindfulness and meditation can significantly impact emotional regulation. Mindfulness includes being completely gift withinside the second and non-judgmentally looking at one's mind and emotions. By becoming more aware of their emotional state, individuals can prevent themselves from being carried away by overwhelming feelings. Meditation techniques, such as deep breathing and progressive muscle relaxation, can help in reducing stress and promoting emotional stability. Empathy and Perspective-Taking: Emotional regulation can be enhanced by developing empathy and perspective-taking skills. By putting oneself in another person's shoes and understanding their emotions and motivations, individuals can foster more compassionate and understanding responses. This shift in perspective can lead to more positive emotional experiences and better communication in interpersonal relationships.

Self-Compassion: Being kind and understanding toward oneself is crucial for emotional regulation. Self-compassion involves treating oneself with the same level of care and support that one would offer to a close friend facing similar challenges. By practicing self-compassion, individuals can prevent self-criticism and harsh judgments, leading to a more nurturing and emotionally balanced internal environment.

Controlling or influencing emotions using thoughts is a skill that can be cultivated with practice and dedication. By becoming aware of cognitive processes, challenging negative thought patterns, and developing empathy and self-compassion, individuals can achieve greater emotional regulation and overall well-being. It is essential to remember that emotional regulation is not about suppressing emotions but rather understanding and managing them in a healthy and constructive manner. Seeking support from mental health professionals can also be beneficial for those who find it challenging to manage their emotions independently. With these tools and strategies, individuals can build resilience and create more fulfilling and emotionally satisfying lives.

CONTROLLING YOUR EMOTIONS USING YOUR WORDS

Language is a powerful tool that can profoundly impact our emotional experiences and well-being. The ability to control or influence emotions using words is an essential aspect of emotional intelligence. By understanding how language affects our emotions and learning effective communication strategies, individuals can develop healthier emotional regulation, improve relationships, and foster a more positive mindset.

Self-Talk and Positive Affirmations: One of the most direct ways to influence emotions using words is through self-talk and positive affirmations. Self-talk refers to the internal dialogue we have with ourselves, which can either be empowering or self-defeating. Negative self-talk can contribute to feelings of anxiety, self-doubt, and sadness. On the other hand, positive affirmations involve deliberately using uplifting and constructive language to boost confidence and motivation. Repeating phrases like "I am capable," "I am resilient," or "I can handle this challenge" can reframe negative thoughts and promote more positive emotional responses. Expressive Writing: Expressive writing is a therapeutic technique that involves writing about one's thoughts and feelings. This process can help individuals gain clarity and understanding of their emotions, enabling them to process and regulate them more effectively. Putting emotions into words can also provide a sense of relief and validation, leading to reduced stress and improved emotional well-being.

Empathetic Communication: The way we communicate with others can significantly impact their emotions and, in turn, influence our own. Empathetic communication involves actively listening to others' feelings and experiences without judgment, criticism, or defensiveness. By expressing empathy and understanding, we can create a safe and supportive environment that promotes emotional connection and mutual respect. Engaging in empathetic communication can help regulate our emotions by fostering positive interactions and reducing conflict. Reframing and Perspective-Shifting: Using words to reframe situations and shift perspectives can be a potent tool for emotional control. Reframing involves looking at a situation from a different angle or finding alternative explanations for events. By doing so, we can reinterpret events in a more positive or less threatening light, leading to a shift in emotional response. For example, instead of saying, "This is a disaster," one can reframe it as, "This is a challenge that I can overcome. Setting Boundaries and Assertive Communication: Establishing healthy boundaries and practicing assertive communication can also influence emotions positively. Being assertive allows individuals to express their needs, desires, and emotions respectfully and directly. This approach can lead to a sense of empowerment and reduce feelings of resentment or frustration. By communicating boundaries effectively, individuals can prevent emotional overwhelm and cultivate more balanced emotional responses.

Humor and Laughter: Humor and laughter are powerful emotional regulators. Using humor in conversations and situations can diffuse tension, lighten the mood, and reduce stress. Laughing releases endorphins, the body's natural feel-good chemicals, which can improve mood and promote emotional well-being. Sharing lighthearted moments and finding humor in challenging situations can help maintain emotional balance and perspective.

In the end, controlling or influencing emotions using words is a skill that requires self-awareness, empathy, and effective communication. By incorporating positive self-talk, affirmations, expressive writing, empathetic communication, reframing, assertiveness, and humor, individuals can develop better emotional regulation and improve their overall well-being. It is important to remember that words have the power to build or destroy, both in ourselves and in our interactions with others. By harnessing the potential of language to promote understanding, support, and emotional growth, we can lead more fulfilling and emotionally satisfying lives.

WAYS YOUR EMOTIONS ARE AFFECTED BY YOUR BREATHING

Breathing is an involuntary bodily function necessary for sustaining life, but its influence goes beyond simple respiration. The way we breathe can have a profound impact on our emotional state and overall well-being. Conscious control of breathing patterns has been a key component of various ancient practices, such as yoga and meditation, and has gained recognition in modern scientific research as well. Understanding the connection between breathing and emotions can empower individuals to regulate their emotional experiences and promote mental and physical harmony.

The Autonomic Nervous System and Breathing: The autonomic frightened system (ANS) controls physical features that arise involuntarily, including coronary heart rate, digestion, and breathing. It is composed of two branches: the sympathetic nervous system (SNS) and the parasympathetic nervous system (PNS). The SNS is responsible for the body's "fight or flight" response during stressful or threatening situations, while the PNS activates the "rest and digest" response, promoting relaxation and recovery. The way we breathe directly influences the balance between these two systems, and thus, our emotional state.

Shallow Breathing and Stress: When we experience stress or anxiety, the body tends to engage in shallow, rapid breathing. This type of breathing is more focused in the chest and involves shorter breaths with limited diaphragmatic engagement. Shallow breathing activates the SNS, releasing stress hormones like cortisol and adrenaline. This physiological response prepares the body for a perceived threat but can also perpetuate feelings of tension and unease.

Deep Breathing and Relaxation: Conversely, deep, slow breathing that engages the diaphragm promotes relaxation and activates the PNS. Diaphragmatic or abdominal breathing involves expanding the belly as you inhale, allowing more air to fill the lungs, and then slowly exhaling. This type of breathing triggers the relaxation response, leading to reduced heart rate, decreased blood pressure, and overall calmness. Deep breathing is a cornerstone of practices like meditation and mindfulness, which help individuals manage stress and regulate emotions. Breathing and Emotional Processing: The way we breathe can influence the processing of emotions in the brain. Neurologically, the amygdala plays a crucial role in emotional regulation and response. Studies have shown that slow, deep breathing can reduce amygdala activity, leading to decreased emotional reactivity. This means that by consciously adjusting our breathing patterns, we can mitigate the intensity of emotional responses to various stimuli. Breathing Techniques for Emotional Regulation: a. Box Breathing: This technique involves inhaling for a count of four, holding the breath for four counts, exhaling for four counts, and then pausing for another four counts before starting the cycle again. It helps create a sense of balance and relaxation. b. 4-7-8 Breathing: Inhale quietly through the nose for a count of four, hold the breath for seven counts, and exhale audibly through the mouth for eight counts. This technique is especially effective for reducing anxiety and promoting better sleep. c. Alternate Nostril Breathing: This technique is common in yoga and involves inhaling through one nostril, closing it off, exhaling through the other nostril, and then switching sides. It can help balance the body's energy and emotions. To conclude, the connection between breathing and emotions highlights the significant role breath control plays in regulating our psychological and physiological states. By practicing mindful and intentional breathing techniques, individuals can influence their emotional experiences positively. Deep breathing activates the relaxation response, while shallow breathing can perpetuate stress and tension. Understanding the power of breath provides a valuable tool for managing emotions and promoting overall well-being, making it an essential skill for maintaining mental and emotional health in daily life.

HOW YOUR SURROUNDINGS INFLUENCED YOUR EMOTIONS

In the intricate dance between the self and the world, the surroundings in which we find ourselves play a profound role in shaping the symphony of our emotions. This classical detail delves into the alchemy of influence, exploring the ways in which our environment weaves its threads into the fabric of our emotional landscape, conducting a harmonious or dissonant composition.

The Ebb and Flow of Nature:with its majestic grandeur and gentle serenity, exerts a captivating influence on our emotions. The embrace of a lush forest or the rhythmic crash of ocean waves can awaken a sense of awe and tranquility within us. Conversely, the barrenness of a desert or the intensity of a storm can evoke feelings of introspection or unease. Nature's symphony stirs our emotions, reminding us of our profound connection to the natural world.

II.**The spaces we inhabit:**the structures we build, and the designs that surround us compose the architecture of influence. The sweeping arches of cathedrals may evoke reverence, while the coziness of a well-lived home can envelop us in comfort. The symphony of emotions is orchestrated by the architectural choices we make, affecting our moods, behaviors, and perceptions of the world.

III. **The Palette of Colors:**Colors, like the artist's palette, paint emotions upon the canvas of our hearts. The warmth of red may ignite passion or intensity, while the calming embrace of blue can evoke a sense of serenity. The vibrant hues of a sunset may fill us with wonder, while the coolness of green may invite us to embrace tranquility. The symphony of colors in our surroundings colors the symphony of our emotions. IV. The Melodies of Sound Sounds, from the delicate whisper of a breeze to the powerful crescendo of music, conduct the symphony of emotions with incredible finesse. The melodies of sound can uplift our spirits, evoke nostalgia, or immerse us in deep reflection. The bustling city streets may stir restlessness, while the gentle lull of raindrops can induce relaxation. Sound, like a skilled conductor, sets the tempo of our emotional journey. V. The Company We Keep The people with whom we share our lives, our companions in the symphony of existence, profoundly influence our emotions. The genuine laughter of friends can spark joy, while the empathetic support of loved ones can soothe pain. The symphony of emotions resonates in the shared experiences and emotional connections that enrich our human experience.

VI. The Weave of Culture: Culture weaves a rich tapestry of influences that shape the emotional tones of our lives. Cultural norms and values dictate what emotions are encouraged or discouraged, shaping the way we express and understand our feelings. From celebrations that ignite jubilation to rituals that honor grief, culture orchestrates the symphony of emotions in unique and profound ways. Conclusion In the grand symphony of emotions, the surroundings act as both conductor and composer, infusing the melody of our lives with varied shades and intensities. From the gentle sway of nature's embrace to the vibrancy of colors and the resonance of sound, the alchemy of influence intertwines with the essence of our being. By embracing the interplay between the self and the world, we learn to harmonize our emotional landscape, allowing the surroundings to enrich our emotional repertoire, and conduct a more harmonious and nuanced symphony of life.

HOW MUSICAL EMOTION IMPACTS YOU

Music has a unique and profound ability to evoke a wide range of emotions in individuals. It has been an integral part of human culture for millennia, used in various settings to express feelings, tell stories, and create connections between people. The relationship between music and emotions is a fascinating field of study that explores how melodies, rhythms, and harmonies can profoundly impact our emotional states and overall well-being.

Empathic Resonance: Music possesses the power to resonate with our emotions in a way that few other art forms can. Certain melodies or lyrics can trigger memories or emotions from the past, evoking nostalgia, joy, or even sadness. The emotional or Empathic resonance of music lies in its ability to tap into our subconscious and elicit strong emotional responses without explicit reasoning.

Mood Regulation: Music can influence and regulate our moods, providing a powerful tool for emotional management. Upbeat and energetic tunes can lift our spirits, boost motivation, and enhance productivity. In contrast, soothing and calming melodies can help us relax, reduce stress, and find comfort during difficult times. The ability to curate playlists tailored to specific emotional needs makes music a readily accessible and effective mood enhancer.

Expression of Feelings and Catharsis: Music provides a safe and expressive outlet for emotions that might be challenging to articulate through words alone. Composing or listening to music allows individuals to channel their emotions and experiences into melodies and lyrics, creating a sense of catharsis and emotional release. This cathartic process can be therapeutic, helping individuals process and cope with complex emotions. Empathy and Connection: The emotional impact of music extends beyond personal experiences. It has the power to create connections and foster empathy among individuals. When we listen to songs that reflect the emotions and experiences of others, we can better understand their perspectives and develop a sense of shared emotional resonance. Music can bridge cultural, linguistic, and societal barriers, uniting people through shared emotional experiences. Neurological Effects: Studies in neuroscience have shown that music activates various regions of the brain associated with emotions and reward systems. Listening to pleasurable music triggers the release of dopamine, a neurotransmitter associated with feelings of pleasure and reward. Additionally, music stimulates the limbic system, which is responsible for processing emotions, memories, and motivation.

Music Therapy: Music therapy is a recognized form of therapeutic intervention that uses music to address emotional, cognitive, and physical needs. Music therapists work with individuals to achieve specific emotional goals, such as reducing anxiety, improving mood, and enhancing emotional expression. Music therapy has been beneficial in a wide range of settings, including hospitals, schools, and mental health facilities.

Coming to a close, the impact of music on emotions is a multifaceted and profound phenomenon. From evoking emotional resonance and regulating moods to providing a platform for emotional expression and fostering connections, music plays a vital role in our lives. Whether as a source of comfort during difficult times or a tool for enhancing positive emotions, music has the power to influence and enrich our emotional experiences in ways that are both deeply personal and universally shared. Its therapeutic potential is vast, making it an essential element of human culture and a valuable resource for emotional well-being.

PART III A GUIDE IN CHANGING YOUR EMOTIONS

Humans naturally experience emotions, which have a significant impact on our daily lives and general wellbeing. While the initial emotions that occur in reaction to diverse situations are sometimes beyond our control, we do have the power to affect and alter how we feel and express those emotions. Changing our emotions requires improving our emotional intelligence and using a variety of coping mechanisms. This manual offers a step-by-step strategy to assist you as you work through the process of altering your emotions and developing a healthier emotional state.

Self-Awareness:

Increasing your self-awareness is the first step in improving your emotional state. Pay attention to how you are feeling and note the feelings you are feeling. Be sincere with yourself about the reasons behind these and the factors that lead to them.

The ability to feel emotions without becoming overwhelmed by them creates a space for conscious emotional control.

Challenge and reframe problematic thought processes that fuel unpleasant emotions using cognitive restructuring. Cognitive restructuring entails replacing unbalanced or negative thoughts with ones that are more reasonable and balanced. For instance, if you frequently over-anxiously imagine the worst-case scenario, try to reframe your thinking by imagining just the best-case scenario.

Practice accepting your emotions:
Recognize that it is normal and acceptable to feel a variety of emotions, even negative ones. Give oneself permission to experience emotions fully rather than repressing or avoiding them. Don't criticize yourself or yourself for feeling certain emotions. Acceptance is a key step in figuring out how to properly alter your emotional reactions.

Create Coping Mechanisms: Arm yourself with effective coping mechanisms to deal with difficult emotions. Get moving, express yourself creatively, or spend time in nature to help you let go of emotional strain. Create a network of people you can talk to about your feelings with and who you can turn to for advice when necessary, such as friends, family, or professionals.

Building social awareness and empathy can help you better comprehend the feelings of others and react to them with more compassion. This awareness can help you respond to others' emotions more skillfully while also controlling your own, which can lead to better emotional regulation in **interpersonal relationships.**

Seek Professional Assistance: In order to change deeply rooted emotional habits, assistance from a professional may be needed. Think about getting help from a counselor or therapist who specializes in cognitive-behavioral therapy and emotional management. An expert can offer you specialized techniques and resources to effectively manage and alter your emotions.

In conclusion, learning how to control your emotions is a process that calls for self-awareness, endurance, and practice. You can learn to control and alter your emotional reactions by improving your emotional intelligence, practicing mindfulness, using cognitive restructuring, and coming up with healthy coping mechanisms. Keep in mind that emotions are a normal aspect of being human and that it is acceptable to feel a variety of emotions. You may create a healthier emotional state and improve your general well-being with dedication and help.

FORMATION OF EMOTIONS

Complex psychological states known as emotions are created by a confluence of biological, cognitive, and social elements. Understanding how our sentiments and responses to diverse events are formed is crucial for understanding how emotions develop. The brain, neurological system, previous experiences, and social factors all play important roles in the complex processes that give rise to emotions. This in-depth book examines how emotions are created and offers insight into the interesting processes that control our emotional experiences.

Emotional Biological Basis:

The biological underpinnings of emotions begin in the brain. The amygdala, hippocampus, and hypothalamus are only a few of the parts of the limbic system that are important in the development and control of emotions. Particularly when it comes to processing emotional reactions, the amygdala plays a key role. When we are exposed to inputs that we judge to be either helpful or detrimental, the amygdala sets off emotional responses that prime the body for action. Dopamine, serotonin, and norepinephrine are neurotransmitters that are important in the development of emotions. These substances have an impact on how we feel and how we behave. Stress or perceived dangers cause the release of hormones like cortisol and adrenaline, which contribute to the "fight or flight" response and influence emotional responses.

Cognitive Evaluation:

Cognitive assessment affects emotions, which are not only reflexive reactions to outside stimuli. Based on our beliefs, experiences from the past, and unique traits, we evaluate and understand events and circumstances cognitively. The emotional reaction that a situation inspires depends on how we understand it. For instance, the same occasion Depending on how a person perceives the scenario cognitively, it may inspire anxiety in one person and exhilaration in another.

Past Experiences and Memory:

Memories and past experiences are important in the development of emotions. The brain stores emotional memories that can be reactivated by similar incidents or circumstances. For instance, hearing a music that has special meaning during a former relationship can evoke feelings of sadness or nostalgia. Our emotional reactions in the present are influenced by the retrieval of emotional memories thanks to the amygdala's association with memory. Social and Cultural Influences: Social and cultural factors have an impact on emotions as well. The way that emotions are expressed and understood within a specific culture is influenced by social norms, values, and expectations. For instance, whereas certain cultures value candor in emotional communication, others may the importance of emotional moderation. Since emotions are frequently expressed and transmitted through social connections, social interactions and relationships with others can also have an impact on emotional experiences.

Developmental Factors: Especially during early life, developmental factors have an impact on how people develop emotionally. Emotional regulation and expression are significantly shaped by interactions with caregivers and early attachment experiences. A child's emotional development and how they later perceive, and experience emotions may be significantly influenced by the emotional milieu in which they are raised.

Cognitive and behavioral influences:

Emotional development is also influenced by cognitive-behavioral processes, such as learned associations and conditioning. For instance, if someone is stressed out in a certain area repeatedly, they could form a conditioned emotional response to that setting. Like how positive feedback and rewards can affect the development of happy feelings connected to actions or experiences. The development of emotions is a complex and dynamic process that is influenced by biological, cognitive, social, and developmental variables. How we feel and react to the environment around us is significantly shaped by the limbic system, cognitive assessment, previous experiences, social interactions, and cultural context of the brain.

Emotions can be affected and controlled using a variety of techniques, such as cognitive restructuring, mindfulness, and social support. They are neither fixed nor unchangeable. We can obtain important insights into our emotional experiences and create effective ways to navigate and regulate our emotions by comprehending the complex processes involved in emotion production.

CHANGING THE WAY, YOU THINK

Our thoughts have a significant impact on our beliefs, attitudes, behaviors, and emotional reactions. Our thought processes and cognitive functions significantly influence how we interpret events and experiences as well as how we perceive the world. Self-doubt, pessimism, and cognitive distortions are examples of negative thought patterns that can harm our mental health and attitude on life in general. Self-awareness, confronting problematic thoughts, and using more kind and upbeat cognitive methods are all aspects of changing the way you think. This manual examines practical methods for altering thought habits and developing a more positive outlook.

Learning to Be Self-Aware:

To start thinking differently, you must first become self-aware. Be mindful of your thoughts and take note of any repeated themes or critical self-talk. Self-awareness entails being able to observe your thoughts without passing judgment, spot any cognitive biases or irrational ideas, and recognize how these thoughts affect your feelings and actions.

cognitive reorganization: An effective therapy method for challenging and changing unhelpful thought patterns is cognitive restructuring. It entails challenging the veracity and accuracy of your negative thoughts and substituting more reasonable and realistic ones. Typical cognitive distortions include the following:

a. **Black-or-White Thinking**: Seeing situations as having just two possible outcomes with no gray area.

b. **Overgeneralization:**Generalizing based on a single

instance or scant information.

c. **Mental filtering:**Concentrating solely on a situation's drawbacks while ignoring its advantages.

d. **Personalization**: Assuming accountability for circumstances beyond your control and placing blame for unsuccessful results.

a. **Catastrophizing:**Exaggerating a situation's possible repercussions and assuming the worst.

You can develop a more uplifting and reasonable viewpoint by confronting these distortions and substituting more sensible ideas.

Practice Positivity in Oneself: Negative or self-critical self-talk should be replaced with helpful and uplifting phrases. Treat yourself nicely and with the same consideration and sympathy that you would extend to a friend going through a similar situation. Repeat uplifting words about your skills, qualities, and potential while you practice affirmations. Positive self-talk over time can increase confidence and self-worth.

Thankfulness & Reframing: Develop thankfulness by emphasizing the positive elements of your life and reinterpreting challenging circumstances. Find possibilities for improvement and lessons learned rather than concentrating on what went wrong. Gratitude aids in turning your attention inward and fosters a more upbeat mindset.

Meditation and mindfulness: To become more conscious of your thoughts and feelings without attachment or condemnation, practice mindfulness. With the use of mindfulness, you can keep an objective eye on your thoughts and spot destructive patterns and emotional triggers. In addition to lowering stress and anxiety, meditation can also foster a sense of clarity and tranquility. **Seek Support and Professional Assistance:**It can be difficult to change your way of thinking, particularly if negative thought patterns are deeply ingrained. Ask friends, family, or support groups for assistance. Additionally, think about seeking advice and tailored cognitive restructuring tools from a mental health expert, like a therapist or counselor.

Results showed that restructuring your thinking is a transformative process that incorporates self-awareness, encouraging self-talk, mindfulness, and cognitive restructuring. You can create a better mentality and enhance your emotional wellbeing by questioning destructive thought patterns and implementing more positive cognitive techniques. Keep in mind that altering your thought process takes time and effort, but with commitment and assistance, you may develop a more upbeat and optimistic attitude on life.

SETTING ASIDE YOUR FEELINGS

As a coping mechanism, putting your emotional responses to a situation or event on hold is known as setting aside your feelings. Although emotions are a fundamental part of being human, there are times when it may be advantageous or necessary to put them on hold in order to complete activities or come to a decision. This article examines the idea of putting sentiments aside, the circumstances in which it might be beneficial, and the potential difficulties and consequences of doing so.

Context and Objectives: It's common practice to suppress your emotions in particular situations in order to accomplish a particular goal. It could be required in circumstances that call for quick decisions, fast action, or professional obligations. For instance, a healthcare worker would need to put aside personal sentiments while treating a patient in a way that ensures unbiased and efficient care. Setting aside your emotions can be a sort of emotional regulation that enables you to control strong emotions and keep them from impairing your capacity for reason and appropriate action. You can avoid irrational responses and keep your composure in stressful circumstances by doing this.

Making Important Decisions: Personal feelings can sometimes impair judgment and result in skewed judgment calls. You may make judgments more objectively by putting your emotions aside and thinking through all the pertinent details and possible outcomes. Focus on Task Completion: When emotions may interfere with productivity, putting aside your sentiments might help you concentrate on finishing activities quickly. It enables you to maintain your concentration on the current work without becoming unduly swayed by emotional sidetracks.

Professionalism:it is frequently necessary to preserve professionalism in workplace environments. Building trust and upholding a positive environment requires exhibiting emotional control and impartiality, whether in the office or other professional settings.

Setting aside your emotions might be helpful in some circumstances, but there may also be potential difficulties and ramifications when doing so:

a. **Emotional Suppression**: Recurringly putting feelings to the side without addressing them can result in emotional suppression, which could have long-term harmful effects on mental health.

b.   **Emotional   Disconnect:**Consistently   repressing emotions over time may result in an emotional disconnect, making it more difficult to access and express emotions when they are needed.

c. **Unsolved Emotions**: Neglecting emotions can lead to unsolved problems that may later reappear and cause more emotional discomfort.

Impact on Relationships: Keeping emotions under check can hinder emotional connection and communication in intimate partnerships, resulting in misunderstandings or emotional distance.

Finding Balance: For emotional well-being, it's important to strike a balance between suppressing feelings when it's required and acknowledging and dealing with them. Recognize that repressing emotions indefinitely is unhealthy because emotions are a legitimate and normal element of human existence. Instead, cultivate emotional intelligence and coping mechanisms to handle emotions well and express them when necessary.

In some circumstances, suppressing your emotions can be a helpful coping mechanism that can help you control your emotions, make wise choices, and concentrate on getting the job done. But it's important to recognize that feelings are a natural part of life and must be dealt with and processed in a healthy way. Try to strike a balance between suppressing emotions when requireA GUIDE IN CHANGING YOUR EMOTIONSd and dealing with them in a healthy way. Encourage emotional health and sustain wholesome relationships.

MAKING YOUR MIND MORE RECEPTIVE TO EXPERIENCING MORE POSITIVE EMOTIONS

Your general well-being and quality of life can be greatly impacted by having an open mind to good feelings. While experiencing negative emotions is a normal part of life, developing an open and responsive mindset to positive feelings can improve your resilience, happiness, and emotional health. This manual explains how to develop a responsive mind that welcomes positive feelings and enables you to live more joyfully, gratefully, and contentedly.

Develop Mindfulness:

Being mindful means paying close attention to the present moment and objectively observing your thoughts and feelings. When you practice mindfulness, you become more conscious of your emotional states, which enables you to appreciate good things when they happen. Additionally, mindfulness enables you to let go of negative thought patterns and rumination, making room for the emergence of more uplifting feelings.

Concentrate on Gratitude: Gratitude is a strong, uplifting emotion that may be developed through deliberate effort. Regularly take some time to think back on the large and little things in your life for which you are thankful. It can be beneficial to educate your mind to concentrate on the good elements of life by keeping a gratitude journal in which you list the things for which you are grateful each day.

Challenge Your Negative Thought Patterns: Your ability to be open to happy emotions can be hampered by negative thought patterns. To develop a more optimistic mindset, challenge and reframe negative thoughts. If you find yourself thinking, "I always mess things up," for instance, try reframing it as, "I may make mistakes, but I also learn and develop from them.

Positive People Around You: Your emotional state can be influenced by the people you spend time with and the material you watch. Surround yourself with people who are upbeat, encouraging, and who make you feel good. Limit your exposure to unpleasant news and other materials that could make you anxious or upset.

Take Part in Joy-Inspiring Activities: Determine the sports that give you joy and schedule regular time to participate in them. pursuing interests, spending time with family and friends, or engaging in activities that correspond with your passions can arouse joyful feelings and encourage an open thinking.

Self-Compassion Exercise: Treat yourself with kindness and compassion. Give yourself the same consideration and education that you would give to a friend. Recognize that it's acceptable to feel a variety of emotions, including negative ones, and that you deserve joy and good times.

Express and Share Feelings of Positivity: The joy and connection can be increased by expressing and sharing pleasant emotions with other people. With loved ones, commemorate accomplishments and landmarks and enjoy happy and grateful moments. This builds social ties and emotional connections while also increasing your personal openness to good feelings.

Make Positive Affirmations: Construct affirmations that speak to you personally and repeat them frequently. happy phrases called affirmations can rewire your brain to reinforce a happy outlook. Use phrases like "I am worthy of happiness and love" or "I attract positivity into my life" when speaking to yourself.

Create a Positive Attitude: Begin each day by creating a positive attitude for the day. Imagine yourself feeling happy and keeping that happiness with you all day long. Setting intentions might help you adopt a positive mindset and open yourself up to more fulfilling situations.

In a nutshell developing a sensitive mind to good emotions requires mindfulness, appreciation, self-compassion, and partaking in enjoyable activities. You may cultivate a mindset that welcomes and embraces joy, happiness, and contentment in your daily life by questioning negative thought patterns, surrounding yourself with positivity, and expressing and sharing positive emotions. Remember that being positive is a skill that can be acquired with practice and intention. By cultivating an open mind, you may improve your mental health and enrich your experience of life as a whole.

MODIFYING YOUR BEHAVIOR TO AFFECT YOUR EMOTIONS

Due to the reciprocal nature of the interaction between behavior and emotions, both our actions and feelings have the potential to affect one another. An effective strategy for managing emotions and promoting emotional wellbeing is to change your behavior. You may improve your emotional experiences by purposefully engaging in certain behaviors that will help you build a happy and emotionally supportive environment for yourself. This traditional section examines practical methods for altering behavior to support emotional wellness and have a favorable impact on emotions.

Exercise: Physical activity has been shown to significantly

improve mood. Exercise increases the release of endorphins, which are natural chemicals in the brain that make one feel good. Exercises like yoga, dancing, or jogging can improve your mood, lower your stress levels, and make you feel better overall. Regular exercise can have a profoundly positive effect on your emotional condition.

To handle stress and anxiety, practice relaxation techniques and incorporate them into your everyday activities. Deep breathing, gradual muscle relaxation, and meditation are all methods that can trigger the body's relaxation response, which lowers levels of stress chemicals and promotes emotional calmness.

Attempt To Engage in Positive Social Connections: Social connections have a big impact on our moods. Be in the company of upbeat, kind people who will lift your spirits and provide emotional support. Participate in social activities that foster a sense of connection and belonging through having meaningful conversations, laughing together, and engaging in group activities.

Accept Kindness: Showing kindness to others can bring about feelings of satisfaction and fulfillment. Perform random acts of kindness, donate your time to an organization you believe in, or undoubtedly provide a helping hand to someone in need. Giving can have a beneficial emotional effect on the donor as much as the recipient.

Establishing healthy habits,such as getting adequate sleep, eating a balanced diet, and abstaining from drugs and alcohol, can have a favorable impact on one's emotional well-being. A body that has received adequate nutrition and sleep is better equipped to handle stress and mental difficulties.

Express Your Gratitude: Gratitude practice has a significant impact on emotional wellbeing. Spend some time every day thinking about and being thankful for the good things in your life. A more upbeat and appreciative mindset can be developed by keeping a gratitude book or by discussing moments of thanks with close friends and family.

Set and Achieve objectives:A sense of success and self-esteem can be attained by setting objectives that are doable and working toward them. No matter how minor they may be, acknowledge your accomplishments and the progress you are making toward your objectives. The path to progress and achievement is frequently accompanied by pleasant feelings.

Limit Negative inner dialogue: Be aware of your inner conversation and correct any negative thinking. In place of self-criticism, practice self-compassion and acknowledge your own strengths. Self-talk that is constructive can raise self-esteem and foster a more favorable emotional climate.

Create a pleasant Environment: Make tangible changes to your surroundings that will encourage pleasant feelings. Your emotional wellbeing will be supported if you surround yourself with happy things, arrange your home in uplifting hues, and create a happy, upbeat atmosphere.

A proactive and empowering approach to emotional regulation involves changing your actions to affect your feelings. You can mold your emotional experiences in a positive way by engaging in physical activity, using relaxation techniques, seeking out supportive relationships, embracing acts of kindness, developing healthy habits, expressing gratitude, setting and achieving goals, limiting negative self-talk, and cultivating a positive environment.

Do not forget that altering behavior is a gradual process requiring perseverance and self-awareness. These techniques can be purposefully incorporated into your daily life to Improve your own and others' emotional landscapes by maintaining your own emotional health.

ALTERING YOUR ENVIRONMENT TO CHANGE YOUR EMOTIONS

Our surroundings have a big impact on how our emotions are shaped and how our general well-being is affected. Our emotional experiences can be greatly impacted by the adjustments we make to our environment. We may effectively influence our emotions and promote emotional well-being by making changes to our surroundings to make them more uplifting, encouraging, and emotionally enriching. This traditional detail investigates methods for adjusting the environment to favorably affect feelings and produce a harmonious emotional landscape.

Reduce Congestion and Disorganization: Stress and overwhelm can be caused by cluttered and unorganized surroundings. Decluttering and organizing your living environment is a good place to start. Establish a neat and orderly environment that encourages relaxation. You can concentrate on the pleasant aspects of life and reduce negative feelings by eliminating unneeded distractions.

Describe the natural elements: Make use of natural elements in your surroundings to promote emotions of tranquility and a sense of connection with the outdoors. A sense of calm and wellbeing can be added with plants, flowers, and natural design. Additionally, being outdoors or having nature-inspired decor indoors can lower stress and boost happy feelings.

Use Colors to Evoke Feelings: Colors have a profound effect on our feelings and disposition. Select hues for various parts of your environment that make you feel good. Use warm, lively hues in areas designated for creativity and social interaction, and soothing blues and greens in rooms intended for leisure. Create a setting that is uniquely yours by using colors that speak to your emotional preferences.

Make a Cozy, Comfortable Space: Establish a place where you can go to unwind and relax. Include blankets, cushions, and soft furnishings to create a cozy and welcoming ambiance. A relaxing environment can serve as a sanctuary, promoting emotional well-being.

Display Happy Memories and Positive Affirmations: Surround yourself with positive affirmations, inspirational sayings, and pictures that bring back pleasant memories. You may improve your mood and promote happy emotions by putting up visual reminders of your successes and goals.

Create a Sound Environment: Sound has a profound emotional impact. To create a peaceful atmosphere, play relaxing music or ambient noises like birdsong or water moving. Instead, listen to upbeat music that makes you happy to increase your energy and foster good feelings.

Limit Your Exposure to Harmful Influences: Watch the media and information you take in. Limit your exposure to unpleasant news and other materials that could make you anxious or upset. Instead, look for inspirational and uplifting stuff.

Fostering positive social ties means fostering them in your surroundings. Be in the company of uplifting, encouraging people who encourage your emotional health. Organize get-togethers and social occasions that foster a sense of neighborhood and belonging.

Make Your Space Your Own: Decorate your space with special accessories and furnishings that have an uplifting emotional impact. Create a space that is consistent with your true self by incorporating components that reflect your interests, hobbies, and values.

It is a transforming and liberating process to change your environment in order to change your feelings. You can influence your emotional experiences and improve emotional wellbeing by decluttering and organizing, incorporating natural elements, using colors strategically, making comforting spaces, displaying encouraging affirmations and memories, curating a sound environment, limiting harmful influences, fostering positive social connections, and personalizing your space. Keep in mind that even seemingly insignificant adjustments might significantly alter your emotional state. Try to intentionally create an atmosphere that encourages joy, contentment, and emotional fulfillment.

DEALING WITH NEGATIVE EMOTIONS: SHORT-TERM AND LONG-TERM SOLUTIONS

Negative emotions are a natural crescendo in the symphony of life that frequently puts our emotional fortitude to the test. These feelings, including rage, grief, fear, and anxiety, can come on suddenly and linger, upsetting our sense of inner peace. A healthy blend of short-term solutions to ease current suffering and long-term tactics to foster emotional wellbeing is necessary to master the art of dealing with negative emotions. This traditional exposition explores the various methods for controlling unpleasant emotions with composure, both at the time they arise and during one's entire life's work.

Temporary Relief Through Short-Term Solutions

It's crucial to have an arsenal of quick fixes to restore tranquility when unpleasant emotions come on suddenly:

Mindfulness Use mindfulness meditation to breathe in the essence of the current moment. We make room to see and comprehend emotions without being consumed by them by mindfully noting them without passing judgment.

Exercises for Deep Breathing:A beautiful adagio of slow, deep breaths can quiet the inner turmoil. Pent-up emotions are released when we exhale, and we are filled with peace as we inhale.

Expressive Writing: Expressive writing is the path to transcendence. Writing down our feelings on paper allows for catharsis, which offers a cathartic release from the depths of our spirit.

Physical Exercise:A little exercise can do the world of good. Endorphins, the euphoric notes of our being, flood our bodies when we workout, dance, or even just take a leisurely stroll. Looking for Support As the cello and violin play in harmony, getting help from friends, family, or a therapist can encourage a pleasing interaction of feelings and viewpoints.

Long-Term Remedies a Musical Symphony of Emotions

We must incorporate long-term fixes into our opus if we are to construct a life with enduring emotional harmony:

Take advantage of emotional intelligence's crescendo, where self-awareness, self-control, empathy, and social skills harmoniously interplay. Understanding and controlling our emotions helps us build resilience to life's dissonant chords.

Cognitive restructuring is the process of rearranging the score of our thoughts. Uncover a composition of optimism by challenging negative thoughts and replacing them with affirming and optimistic refrains.

The practice of thankfulness is an age-old adagio that encourages appreciation for life's benefits even in the face of difficulties. Gratitude helps us see the bright spots that shine through even the darkest circumstances.

Developing Resilience: Accept misfortune as a natural part of life's symphony and embrace the fortissimo of resilience. When we view failures as chances for progress, we get the ability to bounce back after each one like a triumphant symphony.

Taking Part in Meaningful Activities: The sonata of meaningful activities reverberates with contentment. Activities that are in line with our values and passions enhance the fabric of life and bring a deep sense of fulfillment.

The search of emotional harmony is a timeless symphony that necessitates mastery of both long-term cultivation and immediate relief. By accepting the ebb and flow of unpleasant feelings, we can create a harmonious existence that reverberates with elegance and fortitude. We own the power of decision; we can either let negative emotions rule us or lead them in symphonic tune with our inner harmony. As we hone the skill of managing unpleasant feelings, we hone the masterpiece of our life, creating a timeless work of calm and self-awareness.

PART IV WAYS TO IMPROVE EMOTIONS

Emotions are the brilliant colors that the great orchestra of life uses to paint the picture of our existence. Enhancing emotions calls for a skillfully orchestrated combination of virtuoso methods, much like a beautiful symphony. This traditional explanation explains the technique for fostering joyful emotions and promoting emotional health through mellow routines, raising our inner symphony to heavenly heights.

Accept Self-Awareness as the Foundation for Emotional Intelligence

Aware Introspection: Mindful reflection allows us to view our feelings without passing judgment because it is embellished with introspection. We develop clarity and go beyond self-awareness by comprehending their causes and triggers.

Create a journal for your emotions by writing down your feelings. By expressing ourselves honestly and authentically through emotional journaling, we reveal the depth of our emotions.

Develop the universal components of emotional intelligence—self-awareness, self-control, empathy, and social skills—in harmony. Our interactions are enriched by this virtuoso performance, which fosters strong emotional bonds.

Encourage Good Emotions: An Inner Delight Allegro Practice expressing a rhapsody of thanksgiving while appreciating life's symphony of benefits. In order to feel joy, embrace the small pleasures and write daily expressions of gratitude.

Act Kindly: Kindness is a crescendo that resonates with compassion. We change the world into a harmonious symphony of love and goodwill by showing kindness to others.

Look for Happy Experiences: Immerse yourself in happy encounters to fully appreciate life's vivacity. Take part in enjoyable pursuits, whether they involve hobbies, the arts, the outdoors, or deep relationships.

Develop Emotional Resilience The Inner Strength Symphony cognitive reorganization Reorganize your thinking by changing your cognitive processes. Substitute uplifting refrains for dissonant patterns to create harmonic resonance.

Accept setbacks as opportunities for growth: Consider setbacks as opportunities for improvement, like a triumphant symphony emerging from a minor key. Accept obstacles head-on and let them shape us into more resilient people.

Meditation: The calming tones of mindfulness meditation promote emotional composure. We separate from emotional turmoil by embracing the present moment, which leads to tranquility.

Encourage Emotional Bonds: Sonata of Compassionate Bonds

Develop Meaningful Connections: The harmony of fulfilling relationships reverberates. Foster relationships through showing empathy, paying attention, and providing sincere support, creating ties that balance our souls.

Open and honest communication strengthens emotional ties because it is transparent. Openly and receptively expressing feelings promotes compassion and understanding between people.

The verdict

The goal of emotional improvement manifests as a magnificent orchestration as we move through the entrancing symphony of life. We create a symphony of inner joy and emotional well-being by embracing self-awareness, fostering positive emotions, developing resilience, and sustaining emotional connections. We use the baton of our choice to enhance emotions and gracefully conduct our inner song, just as a conductor leads a symphony to perfection. In this classical journey, we develop our emotional virtuosity, bringing the euphonious chords of life's emotions into harmony and creating a masterpiece of calm and contentment.

EMOTIONS AND HOW THEY CAN LEAD YOU IN THE RIGHT DIRECTION

Emotions play the parts of the heart strings, the soul winds, and the percussion that set the beat of our journey in the epic symphony of human existence. Emotions have the capacity to guide us in a variety of ways and are frequently referred to as the erratic muse of our existence. This classic explanation explores the deep relationship between feelings and the road they illuminate, demonstrating how they can serve as our compass for choosing the proper course.

Adopting Emotional Intelligence as a Precursor to Discernment

Self-Awareness: The first step in receiving emotional coaching is becoming self-aware. By being more aware of our emotional landscape, we can develop the ability to understand the nuanced aspects of our sentiments and identify potential directions that are consistent with our genuine desires.

How to Recognize Real Emotions: Real emotions can be recognized by the way they harmoniously interact. By expressing our true feelings, we avoid conflicting notes and embrace the path that is consistent with our fundamental beliefs and objectives.

Emotions as Psychic Messengers: Instinctive Navigation Allegro

Intuition and gut feelings: Gut instincts and intuition function as an innate compass, like a melodic cadence. When emotions are felt, they convey subtle messages that direct us to make choices and do acts that are in line with our true selves.

Passion and Excitement: Our enthusiasm propels us into activities that enliven our spirits. These feelings guide us down the right routes, igniting joy, creativity, and fulfillment like a conductor propelling us onward.

Emotions as Change Catalysts: Transformation's Crescendo. Feelings of discomfort and dissatisfaction serve as a change-signaling cue, much like a symphonic rising. They encourage us to adopt new paths that are consistent with our changing selves as they push us away from stagnation and toward growth.

Fear and Courage: Fear and courage are linked in the symphony of life. While courage, like a triumphant major note, encourages us to take risks and explore new areas, fear, like a minor key, tests us.

Letting Go of Emotions to Improve Empathy: The Art of Human Interaction Compassion and empathy We can connect deeply with others by resonating with their feelings thanks to the ability of empathy. We become tuned into the direction as we empathize.

The lyrical substance that links souls is love, and gratitude is its sincere manifestation. Both feelings nudge us in the direction of goodness, inspiring us to show gratitude and kindness to both ourselves and other people.

Emotions become the ethereal orchestra that directs us in the right way as we move through the symphony of life. We weave a beautiful tapestry of existence by embracing emotional intelligence, understanding the intuitive messages contained in our feelings, allowing emotions to serve as change-catalysts, and cultivating empathy through emotions. Emotions shape our decisions, experiences, and relationships like the conductor of a grand symphony, creating a tune that touches the core of who we are. Through this classical investigation, we learn about the tremendous importance of feelings and the melodic compass. that points us in the direction of our true path, guiding us to a life of contentment, purpose, and tranquility.

THE CAPTURE OF YOUR EMOTIONS

Emotions dance with ethereal grace within the complex symphony of the soul, their melodies weaving the fabric of human existence. The delicate cadence of the heart and the harmonic notes of the mind meet as you capture your emotions, setting off on a profound voyage of self-discovery. This classical explanation explores the crescendos of reflection, the allegro of acceptance, and the adagio of emotional resonance to reveal the art of capturing your feelings.

I. **The Emotive Palette Unveiled:**The Prelude to Introspection. Taking a Self-Reflection Journey Dive into self-reflection like a conductor with his baton. Pay close attention to the subtleties of your emotions and learn to distinguish between the notes that ring out the loudest and the ones that are hidden beneath.

Embracing Vulnerability: Emotions can come to the surface thanks to vulnerability's gentle and poignant andante.

Harmonizing the Melodic Landscape in The Allegro of Acceptance

Accepting a Range of Emotions: The crescendo of acceptance recognizes the range of emotions that exist. Accept the complete spectrum of emotions, from ecstatic highs to melancholy lows, for each captures the core of your human experience.

Allowing Emotional Ebb and Flow: Emotions have a natural rhythm, like the ebb and flow of the waves. Allow yourself to go through the ups and downs, knowing that each wave can bring you to your senses.

The Adagio of Emotional Resonance: Crossing the Depths

Expressive Adagio: The expressive adagio offers a means of expressing one's emotions. Allow your feelings to be expressed, turning the intangible into concrete expressions through music, writing, or painting.

Developing Emotional Intelligence:A master of emotional intelligence cultivates empathy and self-awareness. You gain understanding of the subtleties of your emotions with this enhanced awareness, tuning yourself to the most minute changes in your emotional symphony.

The Conclusion. Acknowledging Emotional Mastery

Harmony & Equilibrium: Aim for harmony and balance in your emotional composition like a master conductor. Accept the dissonant sounds and try to resolve them by being kind to yourself and understanding them.

Accepting Imperfection: Recognize that emotions are not always well-rehearsed, like a timeless adagio. Accept flaws as a natural part of life's symphony and take inspiration from each new development.

You embark on an eternal symphony of self-discovery and emotional resonance in the ethereal voyage of capturing your feelings. Your heart's symphony and the mind's harmony merge as you embrace emotional mastery, contemplation, and acceptance. You are invited to feel the crescendos of happiness, the allegros of enthusiasm, the adagios of reflection, and the fortissimos of strength as the enigmatic symphony of emotions develops. You compose a timeless sonata by capturing your emotions, which represents the depth of your soul and the complexities of human existence and reverberates with sincerity, sensitivity, and openness.

NOT DOING WELL ENOUGH

We find ourselves mesmerized by the ever-evolving melodies of success and failure, achievement and setback, inside the big symphony of life. The idea that we are "not doing well enough" can cause dissonance in our minds and hearts, dragging us away from the rhythmic beat of self-compassion and fulfillment. The numerous aspects of this view are explored in this classical exposition, which leads us to the fortissimo of fortitude and the profound adagio of self-acceptance.

The Unharmonious Notes: The Inner Critic's Crescendo and the Perception of Falling Short Self-doubt and self-criticism are amplified by a turbulent crescendo that the inner critic orchestrates. Its unrelenting search for excellence feeds the sense of inadequacy, leading us to doubt our accomplishments.

Comparisons as a Minor Key: Comparing oneself to others' actions resonates within the minor key of comparisons. Perceived achievements. Such comparisons foster a feeling of inadequacy and hide the genius of our individual journey.

The Allegro of Self-Reflection: Accepting Development and Learning.

Accepting Imperfection: Self-reflection's mastery enables us to recognize imperfection as a normal component of the symphony of life. Accepting our human fallibility gives us the opportunity to develop, advance, and learn.

Learning from Setbacks: When we experience setbacks, we often learn priceless lessons. We can regard them as steppingstones on the path to growth and resilience rather than seeing them as failures.

Embracing Our Worth: The Adagio of Self-Compassion The soft adagio of self-compassion envelops us in understanding and gentleness, as described in The Art of Self-Compassion. We fix the dissonant chords by being good to ourselves as we would be kind to other and "not performing adequately".

The sublime notes of thanks enable us to acknowledge our successes, no matter how modest they may be. Gratitude causes us to change our attention from what is missing to what is already there, bringing harmony into our vision.

The Fortissimo of Resilience: Overcoming Perceived Failures.

Seeing Opportunities in Challenges: The fortissimo of resilience inspires us to view difficulties as chances for personal development. We overcome obstacles with courage and tenacity, like a conductor leading an orchestra.

Valuing the Journey: The resilience story's conclusion serves as a reminder that success isn't just determined by where we end up; it's also determined by the musical journey we go on. Respecting the process generates a feeling of satisfaction and success.

The feeling of "not doing well enough" becomes an integral part of our human experience in the ever-evolving symphony that is life. However, we can conduct a harmonic arrangement that transcends the dissonance of inadequacy by embracing self-reflection and learning, growing self-compassion and thankfulness, as well as embracing resilience and appreciating the process. In this classical investigation, we discover that the feeling that we're "not doing well enough" is just a momentary movement in the symphony of our lives, one that deepens our awareness of ourselves and our ability for development. We learn that the feeling of "not doing well enough" is only a passing cadence in the vast opus of our existence, and the actual magnificence lies as we continue to create our distinctive symphony.

A DEFENSIVE SPIRIT

A defensive spirit appears as a multidimensional element in the vast fabric of human emotions, protecting the soul's weaknesses from the harsh winds of the outside world. This protective attitude is marked by complex notes of self-preservation, fear, and protection, much like a complex symphony. The mystery of a protective spirit is clarified in this classical exposition by examining the fortissimo of self-defense, the andante of self-awareness, and the adagio of fragility.

Self-Preservation's Peak: Securing the Inner Sanctum

The Protection of Fear We are protected from potential injury or hurt by the crescendo of a defensive spirit that emerges from the armor of dread. This protective posture develops as a form of self-defense, much like a knight donning armor before battle.

Limits in the Conductor's role: Setting boundaries serves as the protective spirit's compass. It enables us to keep our emotional balance and defend ourselves against outside influences that can endanger our wellbeing.

Untangling the Roots of Self-Awareness

The Maze of Old Injuries The andante of self-awareness explores the maze of old injuries. We gain understanding of the causes of the protective spirit's emergence by separating the emotional strands that connect our experiences.

Understanding Triggers: Self-awareness is the art of discovering the symphony of triggers that cause a protective reaction. Knowing what these triggers are enables us to deal with them more sensitively and compassionately.

Embracing the Sublime: The Adagio of Vulnerability
The Secret Symphony We are invited to embrace the beautiful nature of being human by the adagio of vulnerability. Vulnerability removes the need for constant defense and opens our hearts to genuine interactions like a moving melody.

The Interplay of Trust: In partnerships, vulnerability creates the interplay of trust. By accepting vulnerability, we make it safe for others to do the same, resulting in the seamless synthesis of empathy and understanding.

Emotional Balance's Finale: Balancing Strength and Sensitivity

Exceptional Self-Reflection: We can tell when the protective spirit benefits us and when it gets in the way of our development thanks to the fortissimo of self-reflection. Self-defense and openness are balanced in a beautiful composition.

Accepting Empathy resonates with the emotional balance's conclusion. We develop a greater awareness of others' feelings when we show empathy for them, balancing our natural tendency to be protective with compassion.

Results showed that, We discover a thorough examination of self-preservation, self-awareness, and vulnerability within the complex symphony of a protective spirit. This defensive attitude permeates all aspect of our lives like a complex composition, influencing how we connect with others and have experiences. We conduct a harmonic orchestra as we accept self-awareness, trust in vulnerability, and strive for emotional balance. By recognizing the defensive attitude. We learn to understand its purpose and know when to let our guard down because it's a natural part of the human experience. Through this classical journey, we solve the mystery of a protective spirit, accepting its complexity with compassion and understanding, and finally creating a spiritual symphony of power, sensitivity, and genuine connection.

ANXIETY AND CONCERN

The poignant duet of anxiety and concern can be found within the complex melodies of the human heart. They add shadows and light to the symphony of the soul, weaving together two melodies that mirror the intricacies of human experience. This classical discourse examines the melody of worry and the cadence of anxiety, pointing us in the direction of the crescendo of fortitude and the adagio of emotional stability.

The Prelude of Unease: The Cadence of Anxiety

The Depressing Notes: Moments of peace are tainted with an unending uneasiness by anxiety, which portrays a melancholy picture. It reverberates around the mental hallways like a menacing nocturne, heightening anxieties and uncertainties.

The Peak of Physical Experience: Physical symptoms of anxiety include a racing heart and shallow breathing. These physical reactions provide a symphony of their own, adding to the emotional upheaval.

The Song of Caring Hearts: The Melody of Concern

The calming lullaby A sweet lullaby of worry reverberates from the depths of caring hearts. It demonstrates our intrinsic ability to sympathize with others and compels us to help.

Concern orchestrates an overture of empathy that links us to the feelings of the people we care about. In this symphony of compassion, we learn to be sensitive to the suffering of others and do our part to lighten their loads.

The Duet's Interaction: Both peace and conflict

Resonating in tandem: Concern and anxiety frequently perform a delicate duet that resonates with our relationships to the outside world. When someone else's well-being is in doubt, anxiety may develop because concern leads us to care profoundly for them.

Resolution and Dissonance Harmony results from accepting and appreciating both worry and anxiety, like in a musical resolve. We can negotiate their interaction with grace by realizing that worry doesn't make anxiety go away, and that anxiety doesn't make worry go away.

Embracing balance: The Adagio of Emotional Equilibrium

Taking Care of Your Emotional Health: Nurturing our emotional wellbeing leads to the adagio of emotional balance. Self-compassion and mindfulness exercises build a solid basis for dealing with worry and embracing concern.

Accepting Uncertainty: The moving adagio exhorts us to accept the unpredictability of life. We find comfort in savoring the present by acknowledging that some issues might not be fixed.

In the symphony of the soul, worry and concern play their intricate duet, influencing our interactions and experiences. Embracing worry enables us to expand the beauty of our hearts outward, establishing relationships with others as we maneuver the cadence of anxiety. We achieve peace both inside ourselves and with the outside world by acknowledging the interaction of these emotions. When we cultivate emotional stability and accept vulnerability and uncertainty as essential elements of the human experience, the crescendo of resilience arises.

Weaving a spiritual symphony of empathy, care, and emotional balance that reverberates throughout our lives, we learn to grasp the depth and complexity of anxiety and concern through this classical journey.

CAREFUL OF WHAT OTHERS THINK OF YOU

The opinions of others frequently encourage us to change our melodies to conform to their expectations in the big symphony of life, echoing like far-off notes. We must, however, maintain a delicate balance between upholding our authenticity and paying attention to the advice of others, much like a master conductor. The allegro of self-awareness, the andante of discernment, and the adagio of self-acceptance are explored in this classical exposition, which leads us to a powerful composition that embraces our individuality while appreciating the worth of other people's perspectives.

Self-Awareness Allegro: Tuning into Your Inner Melody Acknowledging Authenticity Self-awareness' allegro inspires us to accept our authentic selves and listen to the notes of our inner music. We create a timeless composition that expresses our true essence while upholding our genuineness.

How to Develop Emotional Resilience: Self-awareness encourages emotional resilience, much like a conductor navigating turbulent sections. It gives us the ability to respond wisely rather than impulsively by helping us to understand our emotional responses to other people's perspectives.

The Andante of Discernment: Weighing Other Points of View

Differentiating criticism from feedback: We can distinguish between constructive criticism and damaging feedback thanks to the andante of discernment. While constructive criticism typically results from the dissonance of other people's unresolved emotions, damaging feedback might help us improve our composition.

Seeking Wise Counsel: We can seek wise counsel from reliable people, just as a conductor could do when looking for guidance from seasoned musicians. Our ability to make decisions is improved when we consider other people's viewpoints with respect and trust.

Adoring the Symphony of Imperfections: The Adagio of Self-Acceptance

Adagio of Self-Acceptance: The adagio of self-acceptance gently embraces our imperfections. Knowing that perfection is a myth, we allow ourselves to accept our imperfections and use them to create special harmonies.

The sensitive adagio serves as a reminder to appreciate our inner worth over other people's approval. We create a composition that is resistant to outside criticism by practicing self-compassion and acknowledging our innate worth.

The Conclusion: A Harmonized Cadence of Viewpoints

Promoting Compassion and Understanding The conclusion is resonant with compassion and comprehension. By putting ourselves in other people's situations, we are able to understand the reasons behind their viewpoints, which promotes empathy and connection.

Choosing Harmonious Melodies: The grand finale serves as a reminder that we oversee making decisions.

Selectively embracing viewpoints that mesh with our true selves allows us to create melodies in our lives.

How to the caution of various viewpoints compels us to fine-tune our composition with wisdom and discernment in the symphony of life. Weaving a symphony that celebrates our individuality while appreciating the significance of various viewpoints, we perform the allegro of self-awareness, the andante of discernment, and the adagio of self-acceptance. We may harmonize with others while staying rooted in our identity thanks to the culmination of empathy and understanding. We achieve a resonant balance in our life as competent conductors, allowing the perspectives of others to enrich our symphonic journey without distorting our own tune. We discover how to appreciate the complex symphony of self-awareness, discernment, and self-acceptance in this classical inquiry, creating a timeless masterpiece that captures the richness and beauty of our true selves.

PIQUE

Pique arises as a fleeting yet seductive tune within the complex collection of human emotions. It disrupts the harmony of our inner symphony, like an unexpected gust of wind, giving the composition more depth and complexity. This classical explanation walks us through the subtleties of this fascinating feeling by examining the allegro of pique, the andante of introspection, and the adagio of resolution.

The Melody of Pique: The Quick Emotional Arousal

The Sudden Decline: Like a sudden crescendo in a symphony, pique appears out of nowhere. It arouses feelings, amplifying our responses to perceived slights or provocations and causing an internal lively tempo.

The Exuberant Expression Pique takes the form of expressive gestures, such as an arched eyebrow, a sharp comment, or a momentary scowl. It imbues our behavior with a fiery zeal and creates the framework for further investigation.

The Andante of Introspection: Using the Underlying Motifs to Navigate

The Pause for Reflection: We pause to consider the fundamental causes of our anger when the andante of reflection gets going. We try to comprehend the emotions that led to this response as well as the factors that set it off.

The Melodic Roots: Looking inward reveals deeper feelings like hurt, insecurity, or dissatisfaction, which are the sources of our ire. We peel back the layers that make up this intriguing sensation like a master conductor.

The Adagio of Resolution: The Peaceful Consonance

The Quiet Descending: The resolve adagio includes a soft decrescendo that invites us to calm the angry notes of pique. We recognize the fleeting nature of this experience and its part in the larger symphony of our emotions.

The Atmosphere of Empathy As the resolution solidifies, we show empathy for other people and try to comprehend their viewpoints and intentions. This act of kindness unites discordant notes into a melodious unity.

Accepting Renewal and Growth:

Compositional improvement We fine-tune the mix of our emotions in the conclusion. We understand that rage can spur self-awareness, allowing us to hone our emotional reactions and develop emotional intelligence.

The Renewal of Melody We experience a melodious rejuvenation as we embrace the transforming power of reflection and resolution. Pique turns into a growth tool that expands our emotional vocabulary and increases our self-awareness.

Pique is a transient but resonant movement in the symphony of emotions that forms the depth of our experiences. We learn about the complexities of this compelling sensation as we move through the allegro of pique, the andante of introspection, and the adagio of resolution. We choreograph a peaceful outcome that unifies us with our own feelings and with the viewpoints of others by embracing empathy and self-.awareness. We learn about the fleeting beauty of pique in this classical excursion, as well as how it may spark growth and rebirth in the symphony of our souls.

ENVY

Envy appears as a discordant note in the grand symphony of human emotions, throwing doubt on the mellow cadence of contentment. It fires a clamor of yearning and dissatisfaction like a turbulent allegro, dragging us away from the melodies of self-acceptance. This traditional analysis explores the allegro of longing, the andante of contemplation, and the adagio of self-compassion as it delves into the subtleties of jealousy.

The Allegro of Longing: The Soul-Stoking Desires

An increase in desire: The perceived advantages or possessions of others serve as the catalyst for envy, which manifests as a crescendo of want. It ignites our need for what we lack by stirring the embers of longing inside us like a gust of wind.

The jarring symphony When we are pulled to the attraction of other people's possessions, the allegro of longing frequently results in an internal dissonant symphony as we alternate between adoration and coveting.

Untangling the Sources of Discontent: The Andante of Introspection

The Pause for Reflection: We take a moment to consider the causes of our jealousy as the andante of reflection gets underway. We try to comprehend the holes it exposes in us and the vulnerabilities that fuel its resonance.

The musical Reflection: Through introspection, we can peel back the layers of our emotions and go on a musical journey. We understand that jealousy may result from unfulfilled needs, feelings of inadequacy, or social pressures.

Adoring the Symphony of Imperfection: The Adagio of Self-Compassion

Using a gentle descent The self-compassion adagio embraces a gently diminuendo, quieting the envious uproar. We forgive ourselves for the unsatisfactory moments as we realize our flaws and human nature.

The Harmony of Healing Self-compassion promotes a therapeutic internal harmony that calms the dissonance of envy. We support our mental health by being nice and empathic toward ourselves.

The Finale: The Introduction to Development and Gratitude

Compositional improvement We fine-tune the mix of our emotions in the conclusion. We harness the energy of jealousy to advance and grow by understanding it as a motivator for self-reflection.

The Gratitude Song: We celebrate thankfulness by embracing the transformational power of reflection and self-compassion. We find comfort in appreciating the grace of our own journey and the wealth that is there within.

Results showed that Envy is a discordant note that undermines the harmonious composition of satisfaction in the symphony of emotions. We learn about the nuances of envy's resonance as we move through the allegro of longing, the andante of reflection, and the adagio of self-compassion. We arrange a peaceful settlement that aligns us with our emotions and promotes emotional development by embracing self-compassion and gratitude. In this traditional investigation, we explore the dissonant beauty of envy and how it can help us achieve better self-awareness, understanding, and emotional balance. We learn to create a symphony of acceptance, appreciation, and peace within the enormous terrain of human emotions by realizing the transitory nature of envy and embracing self-compassion.

MELANCHOLY

Melancholy arises as a hauntingly beautiful elegy that reverberates throughout the soul in the rich tapestry of human emotions. It produces a depth of emotion that resonates with the core of our being, much like a moving adagio. This classical presentation takes us through the melancholy symphony of the heart by delving into the allegro of introspection, the andante of thought, and the adagio of acceptance.

The Allegro of Introspection: Making Your Way Through the Dark Alleys

The Soft Decrescendo The arrival of melancholy is like a soft crescendo that envelops us in its sweet-sour hug. It evokes feelings of melancholy and nostalgia while subtly nudging us toward reflection.

The Mysterious Flow and Drift We travel on an enigmatic journey as we explore the depths of our emotions as we play the allegro of introspection. We maneuver through the ups and downs of sorrow, revealing its many nuances, like a master conductor.

Embracing the Beauty in Sorrow in "The Andante of Thought"

The Moment for Reflection: We pause as the andante of thought develops to consider the meaning of melancholy. We understand its significance as a moving representation of our humanity and our propensity for intense emotion.

The Andante of Reflection enables us to recognize the bittersweet beauty in sadness. It fills the soul with a soft vulnerability, similar to a gentle rain shower, and connects us to the profound essence of life.

The Adagio of Acceptance: Accepting the Symphony of Emotions.

Using a tender decrescendo, The melancholy tones are calmed by the sweet decrescendo that the adagio of acceptance embraces. We accept the fleeting nature of feelings and let sorrow weave its exquisite symphony without struggle.

The Healing Symphony We find comfort in acknowledging melancholy as a component of the wider symphony of emotions in the adagio of acceptance. We give ourselves access to the regenerative power of emotional expression when we allow ourselves to feel and embrace melancholy.

Overcoming Sadness with Grace

The Resolution of the Composition We fine-tune the mix of our emotions in the conclusion. We understand that sadness has its own special beauty and serves as a reminder of our shared human experience, much like a passing nocturne.

The Gratitude Serenade: We serenade thanksgiving while embracing the transformational power of acceptance. We take comfort in valuing the knowledge and wisdom that sadness imparts, enhancing our emotional symphony.

In the symphony of feelings, sadness stands out as an elegy that resonates through the very core of our beings. We develop a deep understanding of the nuances of melancholy's resonance as we move through the allegro of contemplation, the andante of thought, and the adagio of acceptance. We arrange a peaceful settlement that aligns us with our emotions and fosters emotional healing by embracing acceptance and gratitude. This historical investigation reveals the sad nature and its capacity to connect us to the full range of human emotions. We learn to create a symphony that embraces the totality of life and resonates with authenticity, vulnerability, and profound beauty by appreciating melancholy's sensitive grace and accepting acceptance.

ANXIETY

Anxiety emerges as a turbulent composition that resonates through the heart and mind in the broad symphony of human emotions. It casts a shadow over the tranquil cadence like a crescendo of anxiety. This classical explanation walks us through the complex symphony of anxiety by delving into the allegro of anxiety, the andante of introspection, and the adagio of coping.

The Dissonance Within: The Allegro of Apprehension creates a dissonance within, pulling us away from tranquility. Like a tempestuous storm, it disrupts the balance of emotions, amplifying worries and anxiety. Anxiety begins as a subtle prelude, gradually gaining momentum like a gentle breeze. As it crescendos, it transforms into a whirlwind of apprehension, stirring the mind with a sense of restlessness.

The musical Reflection: Looking inside takes us on a musical journey that reveals the ideas and concerns that fuel worry. We examine the symphony of our minds, identifying the sources of our disquiet, like an expert conductor.

The Adagio of Coping: Embracing Serenity and Resilience, using a gentle descent An anxiety-soothing soft decrescendo is embraced by the adagio of coping. Finding little moments of calm during the storm, we learn to control the intensity of our emotions.

The Symphony of Adaptation Techniques We use a variety of coping mechanisms in the adagio of coping to manage our anxiety. We orchestrate a symphony of resilience, whether through mindfulness, relaxation techniques, or asking for help.

The Symphony of Emotion: Compositional improvement We fine-tune the mix of our emotions in the conclusion. We are aware that anxiety, like a transitory trend, can teach us important truths about ourselves.

The Self-Compassion Serenade We sing a song of self-compassion while embracing the transformational potential of coping. Recognizing that worry is a normal aspect of being human, we can be kind and compassionate to our feelings.

In the symphony of emotions, worry stands as a turbulent composition that threatens the tranquility's harmonious equilibrium. We get a deep understanding of the resonance of anxiety as we move through the allegro of apprehension, the andante of contemplation, and the adagio of coping. We choreograph a peaceful settlement that aligns us with our emotions and supports emotional well-being by adopting coping mechanisms and self-compassion. In this traditional investigation, we learn about the transitory nature of anxiety and how it can help us become more self-aware, resilient, and personally developed. We learn to create a symphony that embraces the ebb and flow of emotions, resonating with honesty, strength, and inner harmony by admitting anxiety's presence and adopting coping techniques.

DELAY

Delay, which is frequently overshadowed by its more well-known equivalents, courage and action, appears as a quiet yet profound virtue deserving of reflection in the broad fabric of human existence. This traditional detail aims to delve into the core of delay, exposing the grace that lies inside its patient embrace and the knowledge it bestows upon the human spirit.

The Deconstruction of Haste

The art of delay continues to be a disappearing gem of thought in a world where the temptation of speed is king. As the poet once observed, "Haste makes waste," as opportunities are missed and mistakes are multiplied in the haste. Delay, in contrast, allows deeper insights to develop as it unfolds like a rose's delicate petals, exposing the beauty of each moment.

The Intentional Pause

Delay gives the gift of a thoughtful pause in the middle of life's tumultuous clamor. It provides the opportunity to take a breath, reflect, and consider the effects of one's actions. The thoughtful person understands that true beauty does not come from hasty brushstrokes but rather from the meticulous contemplation of each stroke's composition, like an artist at their easel. purpose.

Thought and Wisdom

The strands of meditation and knowledge are sewn into the fabric of delay. One is given the chance to look into the mirror of their thoughts and feelings as they choose not to act immediately. This introspection deepens comprehension and gives rise to insights. The unripe fruit matures, and the foundation of sagacity is laid in the embrace of delay.

The Patience Tiles

Like how a beautiful mosaic comes together piece by piece, patience takes time to unveil all of its intricate details. The fervent proponent of delay comes to see the beauty of life's steady progression, appreciating both the road and the destination equally. Each instant is a tile in the constantly changing mosaic.

The Strength of Calm

The power of serenity resides inside the heart of delay. It mirrors the chaos of existence while staying undisturbed, like a serene lake reflecting the world above. The soul veiled in delay finds tranquility in confusion, a haven of quiet amidst the raging storms of life.

The Symphony of Anticipation

Delay is a symphony of anticipation rather than just an empty space. It creates a crescendo of eagerness that intensifies the eventual moment of action by tuning the heart to the song of hope. Delay brings the soul closer to the point of accomplishment, boosting the delight of satisfaction, much like a bow poised on strings.

Determination's Dance

Delay and fate dance together in the grand dance of destiny. The most beautiful moments in life frequently occur just when they are supposed to, never a second early or a second late. Destiny is not a matter of chance; it is a question of decision, as the wise philosopher once stated. One is able to make decisions with wisdom and clarity while also embracing their individual path with courage and conviction thanks to delay's gentle counsel.

Summary, delay crafts the fabric of existence with unending patience and accuracy, much like a master craftsman. It is a mysterious quality that is both a source of strength and a time of calm. The human spirit learns about the power of reflection, the beauty of tranquility, as well as timing. May we take a moment to pause, take a deep breath, and tune our hearts to the symphony of delay amid the clamor of life for it contains the timeless elegance of a life lived intentionally and wisely.

FEW INSPIRATIONS

Some inspirations blaze like eternal flames within the vastness of human experience, illuminating the road of life with their bright glow. Through an examination of their everlasting relevance and the transforming influence they have on the human spirit, this classical detail aims to capture the essence of these select few inspirations.

The Magical Flame of Creativity

The spark of creativity, an ethereal power that fires the soul and propels it to create beauty and invention, is the essence of human existence. Creativity transcends the commonplace, raising humanity to new levels of expression and comprehension, whether via the artistry of a painter's brush, the poetry of a poet, or the brilliance of a scientist's discoveries. Being able to co-create with the universe is fundamental to what it means to be human and a gift from God.

The radiant flame of love

The ever-burning flame of love has the capacity to mend broken hearts, bind up wounds, and unite divided souls. Love emanates warmth in all its manifestations, including romantic, familial, and platonic, forging profound connections while nourishing the spirit with kindness and love. The flame of love teaches us to reach out with empathy, to treasure precious moments, and to accept the vulnerability that comes with opening our hearts to others.

The Wisdom's Leading Light

Through the millennia, humanity has been led by wisdom, an enduring flame that burns with wisdom and insight from the past. It springs from the accumulated knowledge of sages and academics, illuminating the paths of individuals who aim to find their way through life's maze. By fostering discernment and clarity, the spark of wisdom empowers us to make wise choices, learn from our errors, and go beyond the confines of our own personal viewpoints.

A Glimmer of Hope

Even in the most dire situations, hope endures as a radiant spark that won't go out. It offers comfort to worn-out hearts and the power to triumph over hardship, acting as a beacon of light amid hopelessness. The flame of hope inspires courage because it serves as a constant reminder that, despite the most dreadful situations, there is always a chance for rebirth and development.

Knowledge's Illumination

The search of truth is stoked by the dazzling flame of knowledge, which enables humanity to broaden its horizons. It serves as the cornerstone upon which progress is constructed, encouraging creativity, comprehension, and the development of our collective awareness. The pursuit of information inspires us to pursue knowledge with a never-ending curiosity and an unwavering commitment to the search for enlightenment.

The respect for gratitude

Our lives are made more abundant by gratitude, a soft flame that warms the heart with admiration and humility. It inspires us to be grateful for all of life's benefits, big and little, and to realize how others have improved our lives. The flame of thanksgiving fosters contentment and fosters a closer connection to the richness and beauty of existence.

The Magnificence of Courage

We are empowered to face our anxieties and meet problems head-on by the strong flame of courage that burns within us. It is the flame that enables us to overcome our limitations, to face challenges head-on, and to take courageous strides in the direction of our goals. The spark of bravery feeds fortitude.

These few inspirations blaze through the fabric of life like unquenchable flames, blazing the path of humanity with their bright light. Each has the potential to enrich our lives, transcend the ordinary, and give our days meaning and purpose. May we treasure and cultivate these inspirations, allowing them to blaze brilliantly within us and serving as our guides as we go through the limitless depths of human experience.

CONCLUSION

In "Conquer Your Emotions," the author masterfully navigates the intricate landscape of human emotions, providing readers with invaluable insights and practical strategies to gain control over their inner world. Throughout the book, the significance of emotional intelligence is emphasized, and the journey towards self-awareness and self-regulation is skillfully illuminated.

The conclusion of this transformative work echoes a resounding message of empowerment and growth. It reminds readers that while emotions are an inherent part of being human, they need not dictate our actions or dictate the course of our lives. Through understanding the nuances of emotions, embracing vulnerability, and fostering empathy, one can forge a path towards emotional mastery.

The author's encouragement to embrace emotions as messengers, rather than obstacles, unveils the potential for profound self-discovery and personal development. By delving into the depths of their emotional landscape, readers are beckoned to confront their fears, break free from destructive patterns, and cultivate a newfound sense of inner strength and resilience.

The book's conclusion serves as an invigorating call to action, motivating readers to embark on a journey of self-transformation with determination and courage. It resonates with the promise that by conquering their emotions, readers can lead more fulfilling lives, form healthier relationships, and navigate life's challenges with grace and poise.

In essence, "Conquer Your Emotions" not only illuminates the importance of emotional intelligence but equips readers with the tools necessary to wield their emotions as instruments of growth and self-empowerment. It leaves a lasting imprint on the reader's psyche, inspiring them to embrace their emotional authenticity and embark on a lifelong journey towards emotional mastery. As readers close the final pages of the book, they do so with a renewed sense of purpose and an unwavering commitment to conquer the vast terrain of their emotions.